Look
at the
Weather

Look
at the
Weather

Britta Teckentrup

Translated and adapted
by Shelley Tanaka

Owlkids Books

We all share the same air and the same sun. The wind, rain, and clouds know no borders. They move around the globe, bringing weather fair and foul.

The weather is different in every spot on the earth, whether you're at the seashore, on the plains, in the mountains, or closer to the poles or the equator. It changes with the passing of the seasons, and everyone experiences it a little differently. Some people prefer cool weather; others like it warm.

Sometimes we even yearn for bad weather. We might long for a cleansing storm so we can smell the summer rain. We want to catch snowflakes on our tongues, feel a brisk wind at our backs ...

Every day, weather plays a part in our lives. It affects the foods we eat, the clothes we wear, the homes we live in, and the things we do for fun or for work. It even affects how we feel.

We look at a snow-hushed landscape and feel calm. We watch the sun sparkling off the waves at the beach and feel happy. We walk into a cool dark forest and feel ... what?

We have such a strong connection to weather, we can't help but wonder about it. What is it? Where does it come from? What makes it change?

What do you wonder about the weather?

I

Sun

We can't imagine our planet without the sun. The sun gives plants the energy they need to grow, and without plants, there would be no animals. Humans would not exist without the sun's light and warmth.

There would be no day or night without the sun. No spring, summer, winter, or fall. No wind, no rain, no clouds.

Without the sun, there would be no weather.

Have you ever seen a glorious, clear summer sky and wondered why it is so blue?

Sunlight is made up of all different colors of light. When sunlight hits the earth's atmosphere, the dust and gas in the air scatter the light in all directions. Blue light is scattered more than the others, and that is what we see.

What is your favorite shade of blue? Steel blue? Powder blue? Baby blue? True blue?

See that airplane way up in the sky? Imagine looking out the window of that plane at the clouds below. They always look white from above because they are made up of tiny drops of water or ice that reflect the sunlight hitting them.

That plane is making its own long, thin cloud. Its engine is burning jet fuel, and the water vapor it produces turns into tiny ice crystals high in the atmosphere.

Look at these clouds. Some look whispery and barely there.

Others are puffy, like giant fleecy cotton balls. The big puffy ones are called cumulus. Cirrus clouds are long and wispy, floating higher up in the atmosphere.

Clouds act like beach umbrellas, keeping out some of the sun's radiation and helping to cool the earth ... and us!

Clouds move with the wind and change shape, even as you look at them.

What do you see? A herd of white sky creatures? Which way are they moving?

Have you ever thought about where clouds come from? The sun plays a part in how they form. Its heat causes water on the earth's surface to evaporate. The water vapor rises high in the air, where temperatures are cooler, and condenses into clouds.

When clouds spread out and turn into a thick gray veil,

wet weather may be on the way.

If the sun comes out while rain is
falling, the sunlight hits the raindrops,
which act like prisms. They split the
sunlight into all its colors—the colors of
a rainbow! If you move, the rainbow will
appear to move, too, which is why you
will never find that pot of gold that is
supposed to lie at the end of it.

When the sun sets and the evening clouds turn pink,

the sky can look bluer than blue.

Sometimes the sky can be many colors at once. Blue, gray, yellow, pink, and white.

Have you ever watched the early morning sky turn from night to light as the sun peeks over the horizon? How many colors can you see?

The evening sky, now that's something to see. The setting sun spreads its golden light over the ground. Like syrup? Like fire? When you close your eyes, can you still feel the sun's light?

"Red sky at night, sailor's delight." People have long believed that a rosy sunset means fair weather the following day.

Have you ever seen a sunset that seemed to fill the sky like a blanket of fire? Was that colorful sky a sign of good weather?

When the sun disappears, dusk sets in. The stars come out, the moon rises in the sky, and the planet Venus may appear. It gleams in the western sky

for a couple of hours after sunset, and again in the eastern sky just
before dawn.

The stars, the constellations, and the fuzzy white band of the Milky Way are easiest to see when the air is clean and dry and there is no artificial light.

Look out your window at night. What can you see? Turn out your lights. Do the stars look brighter?

Moonlight is weaker than sunlight because the moon only reflects the light from the sun. Even so, a full moon is bright enough to light our way.

Can you see a halo around the moon? What does it mean? Is it a sign of wet weather?

Does your world look this magical in the moonlight?

Imagine walking through the forest as the moon disappears and the sun comes up, spreading warmth and light. Take a deep breath. Can you hear the rustling of birds, the scurrying of small animals? Can you imagine plants pushing their way through the soil?

Life is stirring all around you in the dawn. Can you smell it? Can you hear it?

The sun's warmth stirs the air, too. As air heats up, it rises.

When warm air rises, cooler air rushes in to take its place.

That's wind.

The grain fields have turned yellow, and the sun sits high in the sky. These are the hazy, lazy days of summer.

Where are those birds going? Why are they in a hurry?

If it's too hot, some people seek shelter in the woods. The needles and leaves of the trees keep out the sunlight, and the ground stays moist. Streams flow and springs bubble, and the air is nice and cool.

High up on the hill, thick clouds are gathering. It's still clear in the valley down below, but for how long?

The air is thick and muggy. It's as if nature is holding her breath.

Is a storm brewing?

II

Rain

In a way, the sun is responsible for the rain, too. The sun's warmth makes water evaporate, changing it from a liquid to a gas called water vapor. The water vapor rises into the atmosphere, where the wind may carry it long distances.

When it reaches the cold air high in the sky, the vapor condenses into tiny water droplets that build up to form a cloud. When enough of these droplets come together, they are too heavy for the air to hold. So the drops fall to the earth as rain.

Does rain make you want to run for cover?

Or does it make you want to jump and splash in the puddles?

Some people love to feel the rain on their face. They breathe deeply to smell the rich, dark scent of wet earth and laugh as their boots sink into soft, moist mud.

Do you?

Warm summer rains can seem almost golden ...

... while autumn showers can make
the leaves and yellow grass shimmer
until the world looks bright.

But when heavy rain falls from thick gray clouds, the day can turn as dark as twilight.

Sometimes water vapor condenses in the cool of the night, forming a very fine cloud that reaches the earth and surrounds us with early morning haze—in the city and ...

... on the beach, all misty and still.

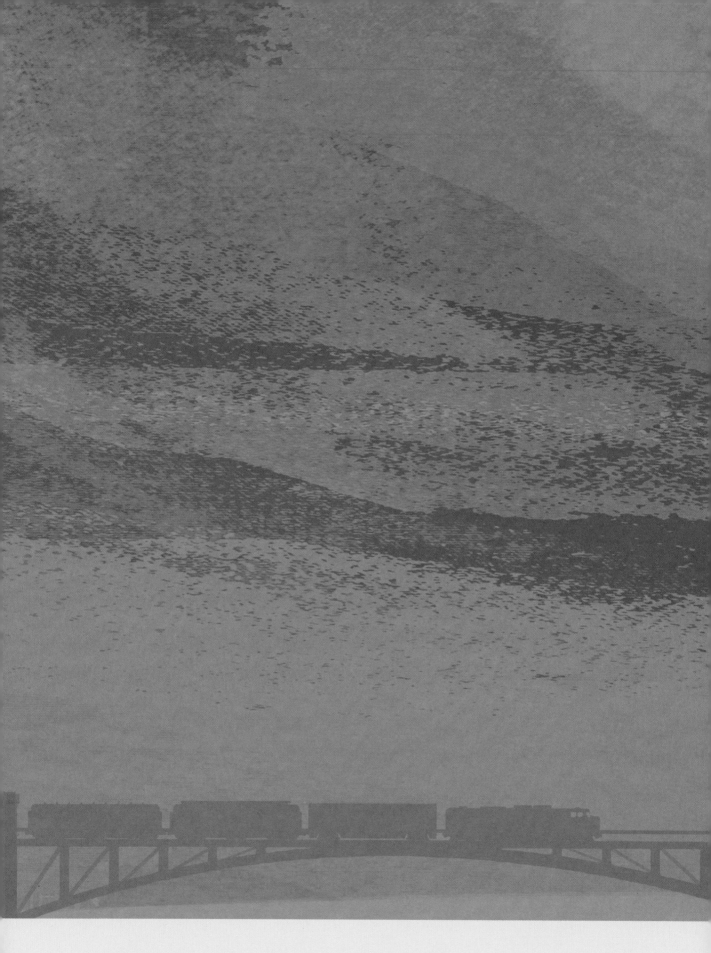

Sometimes that haze thickens and settles in for a while as fog, lingering over

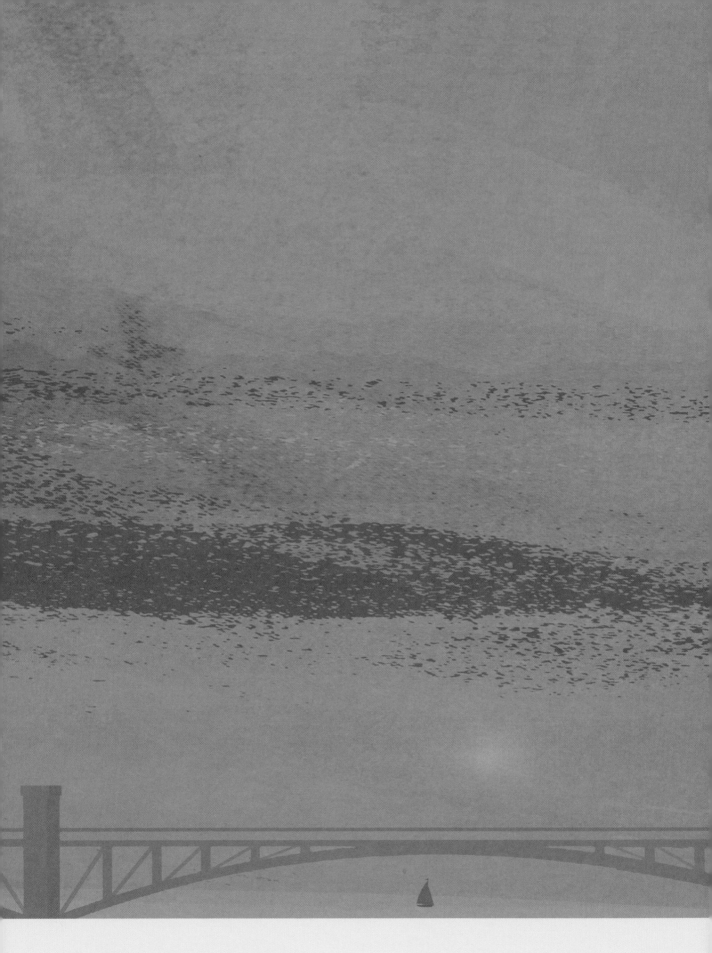

valleys or large bodies of water.

If the mist is very heavy, it can feel like drizzle—rain that's composed of tiny water droplets.

When rain falls for days, it can feel as though the world will be gray and wet forever.

But wait ...

The moon is rising behind the clouds. Can you see it gleaming on the choppy water?

Soon a radiant moon and a sprinkling of stars light up the land.

And the day dawns bright and clear. The air smells fresh and clean—

even in the city!

Birds stretch their wings and drift on the fresh breezes.

Have you ever wished you could soar through the crisp, bright sky with them?

III

Ice and Snow

When water droplets cling to tiny dust particles high up in the cold atmosphere, they create ice crystals that can join together and become heavy enough to fall to the earth. In the warmer air near the ground, the crystals stick to each other, forming snowflakes.

But even before the first snow falls, late autumn often brings frost. When the air cools at night, the water vapor in the ground becomes dew. If the dewdrops freeze where they cool down most quickly—on blades of grass, on rooftops, or on the surface of the soil—they form tiny ice crystals.

In the morning, the whole landscape can be covered with frost.

Winter is on its way!

Sometimes you can almost smell the snow before it comes, as the clouds

gather and the air becomes damp. Soon the first flakes will fall.

The wind blows the snow just as it blows the rain. Keep your head down when it gets too strong!

When temperatures hover around the freezing point, snow and rain mix together to form sleet, and things can get slippery!

At night, the city lights are reflected in the slushy streets.

Can you see the sleet bouncing off the pavement? Can you hear the sound of cars sloshing through the puddles?

If a warm day brings rain in the middle of winter, the water will freeze quickly on the cold ground.

Be careful! Cars skid on black ice, and people slip on icy sidewalks.

Snowflakes reflect almost all the light that hits them. That's why snow looks white, even at night.

And when a fresh blanket of snow covers the ground, the world
suddenly seems peaceful and quiet.

Sometimes a snowy landscape looks as though it could go on forever.

And in the shimmery winter light, it can be hard to make out where

the earth ends and the sky begins.

It would be easy to get lost. Yet the birds always seem to know where they're going.

Then the clouds part, and the snow begins to glisten under the clear blue sky.

A crisp day on a frozen lake. That's ice-skating weather!

First only a thin sheet of ice appears. It floats on the lake's surface because ice is lighter than water. As the frigid days continue, the ice grows thicker and expands. Soon it will be thick enough to walk and skate on.

Up in the hills, the white landscape and the white sky blur together, and bumps in the terrain aren't always visible. Skiers, pay attention!

The meadows and lakes may be covered with snow, but the forest floor is still dark because the canopy of evergreens and branches prevents the snow from reaching the ground.

Still, a few snowflakes drift in, sparkling in the dim light.

A hush seems to fall along with the snow. The air trapped between the ice crystals muffles every sound like a thick blanket. Snow acts like a blanket on the land, too, keeping the ground below warmer than the air above.

When snow softly covers the world outside, does it make you want to snuggle in a blanket of your own?

In the winter, the sun sometimes has trouble penetrating the layers of mist that settle over lowland areas.

But the sun is always there, just waiting for a fresh breeze to stir the air.

Can you see it behind the haze?

Soon the sun will beam out of a deep blue sky, making the snow sparkle like a thousand diamonds.

Will there be more snow? It's already quite deep, and walking is difficult for everyone.

Everything is quiet in the winter woods.

Is it the calm before the storm?

Is it time to seek shelter?

IV

Extreme Weather

Extreme weather feels like someone turned up the volume on our regular weather, creating scorching heat waves, gale-force gusts, and torrential downpours. Sometimes, many kinds of weather happen at once, causing tremendous confusion.

Climate change, which occurs as human activity warms the planet at an unnaturally fast pace, means extreme weather events are becoming more frequent.

Thunderstorms happen when warm and cool air masses meet and mix together quickly in the clouds. The fast-moving air can create electrical charges that are released as flashes of lightning. The air around the lightning is swiftly

heated, and when it expands, we hear thunder rumble and boom. The thunderclouds swell with moisture. Soon the sky will open its floodgates ...

Severe thunderstorms are more intense than typical storms. They unleash downpours and gusts that can be damaging and dangerous.

It's time to go indoors!

Have you ever seen ice fall from the sky on a warm summer day? That's hail, and it's a sign that a thunderstorm is on its way.

Hail is caused when the wind sweeps raindrops up into higher, cooler parts of a cloud before they get a chance to fall. They freeze in the cold air. When the ice droplets begin to fall, sometimes the wind catches them and sweeps them to the top of the cloud again. They can cycle up and down inside the cloud several times, adding layers of water and ice as they go.

Eventually, the ice balls become too heavy for the wind to carry upward, and they fall as hail.

Hailstones are usually the size of peas or marbles, but sometimes they are much larger. Can you imagine hail as big as chicken eggs?

Sometimes extreme weather brings so much rain that the ground cannot hold it all.

Rivers and streams swell. Their fast-flowing currents sweep away everything that stands in their path—trees, bridges, cars, and houses.

Ponds and lakes can rise and overflow their shores, flooding low-lying areas.

shore. The birds know it is time to find shelter, too.

Clouds race across the sky, the wind whistles, and the waves spray high.

Will this bird be caught in the storm?

Huge, swirling storm clouds the size
of cities can form over the oceans
in warm weather. These extreme
storms are called hurricanes when
they form over the Atlantic Ocean,
and typhoons when they form over
the Pacific Ocean.

When they reach the shore, they
batter coastlines with driving rains,
violent winds, and pounding waves.

The fiercest storms of all are born not over water but far inland. Funnel-shaped tornadoes, or twisters, can form in minutes with the force of a

speeding freight train. The spinning column of wind cuts a vicious path
across the land, sweeping up cars, trees, and houses as if they were toys.

In the Far North, cold snaps and blizzards can arrive just as suddenly.

Even large ships can be trapped by pack ice, high winds, and drifting snow.

But not all extreme weather events rush in.

Droughts, which are long periods without rain, happen slowly. Lakes and rivers shrink, and plants wither. Everything feels dry and thirsty, desperate for a drop of water. One little spark can set off a raging forest fire, the trees lighting up like tinder.

Will climate change bring longer spells of dry weather and lead to more intense forest fires?

Will we see more storms of all kinds?

Will extreme weather events become more common and widespread as the planet continues to warm and climates continue to change?

Look at the sky. Look at the weather.

What do you see? What do you feel?

Glossary

ATMOSPHERE The blanket of air that surrounds the earth.

BLACK ICE A thin layer of ice that can be difficult to see on surfaces such as roads and sidewalks.

CLIMATE CHANGE The overall change in typical weather patterns around the world, caused by rising temperatures.

CIRRUS A light, wispy cloud.

CONDENSE To change from a gas to a liquid.

CONSTELLATION A named group of stars, such as the Little Dipper or Orion.

CUMULUS A puffy, cottony cloud.

CURRENT Water or air moving in one direction.

DAWN The lightening sky as the sun rises.

DEW Tiny drops of moisture that form on grass and leaves at dawn.

DRIZZLE A light, misty rain.

DROUGHT A long period without rain.

DUSK The darkening sky as the sun sets.

EVAPORATE To turn from a liquid to a gas because of heat.

GUST A sudden, intense burst of wind.

HAIL Frozen drops of rain.

HAZE A thin mist.

HORIZON The line where the land meets the sky.

ICE CRYSTAL A tiny, flat piece of ice with straight edges. Clumps of ice crystals form snowflakes.

MILKY WAY The name of the galaxy to which the earth belongs. It can sometimes be seen in the night sky as a pale, white cluster of stars.

MUGGY Warm, damp air that feels close and heavy against your skin.

PACK ICE A mass of large ice chunks floating in the sea.

PRISM A piece of glass with many flat sides that refracts, or bends, light.

RADIATION (SUN) Energy from light and heat.

SLEET A mix of rain and snow or hail.

TWILIGHT The soft, dim light from the sky just before sunrise or just after sunset.

WATER VAPOR Water in a gas form instead of a liquid. Steam is an example of water vapor.

Author's Note

For centuries, artists have observed the weather and noticed its connection with human emotions. Landscape painters express and inspire feelings by carefully depicting weather in their art.

This book owes a debt of gratitude to these painters—from Titian to Turner, Caspar David Friedrich, Claude Monet, Vincent van Gogh, and David Hockney.

Text and illustrations © 2015 Verlagshaus Jacoby & Stuart GmbH, Berlin, Germany
Translation © 2018 Owlkids Books
Translated and adapted by Shelley Tanaka
The translation of this work was supported by a grant from the Goethe-Institut.

Owlkids Books acknowledges the financial support of the Canada Council for the Arts, the Ontario Arts Council, the Government of Canada through the Canada Book Fund (CBF) and the Government of Ontario through the Ontario Media Development Corporation's Book Initiative for our publishing activities.

Published in Canada by
Owlkids Books Inc.
10 Lower Spadina Avenue
Toronto, ON M5V 2Z2

Published in the United States by
Owlkids Books Inc.
1700 Fourth Street
Berkeley, CA 94710

Library and Archives Canada Cataloguing in Publication

Teckentrup, Britta
[Alle Wetter. English]
    Look at the weather / by Britta Teckentrup ; translated by Shelley Tanaka.

Translation of: Alle Wetter.
 ISBN 978-1-77147-286-9 (hardcover)

    1. Weather--Juvenile literature. 2. Climatic changes--Juvenile literature. 3. Environmentalism--Juvenile literature.
I. Tanaka, Shelley, translator II. Title. III. Title: Alle Wetter. English.

QC981.3.T4313 2018   j551.5   C2017-904441-9

Library of Congress Control Number: 2017946101

Manufactured in Dongguan, China, in October 2017, by Toppan Leefung Packaging & Printing (Dongguan) Co., Ltd.
Job #BAYDC47

A   B   C   D   E   F

Publisher of Chirp, chickaDEE and OWL
www.owlkidsbooks.com | Owlkids Books is a division of Bayard CANADA

Powerful storms often brew over the ocean. Waves begin to swell as a storm approaches. It's time for sailors to pull in their sails and head for

Every day, every part of our lives is affected by weather. Think about how it affects you.

Go outside. Breathe in the fresh air. Feel the breeze on your skin.